HOW DO WE KNOW ABOUT MARCO POLO?

Marco Polo lived from 1254 to 1324, and his famous journey to China and other Asian countries lasted from 1271 to 1295. In 1298, Marco was captured during a naval battle between his home city of Venice and the nearby city of Genoa. While in prison, he dictated the story of his travels to another prisoner, Rustichello da Pisa.

Rustichello was a writer of romances—adventure stories about knights and ladies. Did he "improve" Marco's story to make it more exciting? Well, perhaps he did, but most experts think the story that Rustichello wrote down is pretty accurate.

Rustichello probably wrote the story in French at first—because romances were usually written in French—but it was soon translated into many other languages. The oldest copies of the book are manuscripts (handwritten copies), because printing was not yet known in Europe.

Printing had already been invented in China—but, strangely enough, Marco doesn't mention it in his story!

Author:
Jacqueline Morley studied English at
Oxford University. She has taught English and
history and now works as a freelance writer.
She has written historical fiction and nonfiction for
children.

Artist:
David Antram was born in Brighton, England,
in 1958. He studied at Eastbourne College of Art
and then worked in advertising for 15 years before
becoming a full-time artist. He has illustrated
many children's nonfiction books.

Series creator:
David Salariya was born in Dundee, Scotland.
He has illustrated a wide range of books and has
created and designed many new series for
publishers in the UK and overseas. David
established The Salariya Book Company in 1989.
He lives in Brighton with his wife, illustrator
Shirley Willis, and their son Jonathan.

Editor: **Stephen Haynes**

Editorial Assistant: **Mark Williams**

**PAPER FROM
SUSTAINABLE
FORESTS**

© The Salariya Book Company Ltd MMIX
No part of this publication may be reproduced in whole or in
part, or stored in a retrieval system, or transmitted in any form or
by any means, electronic, mechanical, photocopying, recording,
or otherwise, without written permission of the publisher. For
information regarding permission, write to the copyright holder.

Published in Great Britain in 2009 by
The Salariya Book Company Ltd
25 Marlborough Place, Brighton BN1 1UB

ISBN-13: 978-0-531-21327-8 (lib. bdg.) 978-0-531-20518-1 (pbk.)
ISBN-10: 0-531-21327-7 (lib. bdg.) 0-531-20518-5 (pbk.)

All rights reserved.
Published in 2010 in the United States
by Franklin Watts
An imprint of Scholastic Inc.
Published simultaneously in Canada.

A CIP catalog record for this book is available
from the Library of Congress.

Printed and bound in China.
Printed on paper from sustainable sources.

You Wouldn't Want to Explore with Marco Polo!

Written by
Jacqueline Morley

Illustrated by
David Antram

Created and designed by
David Salariya

A Really Long Trip You'd Rather Not Take

Franklin Watts®
An Imprint of Scholastic Inc.
NEW YORK • TORONTO • LONDON • AUCKLAND • SYDNEY
MEXICO CITY • NEW DELHI • HONG KONG
DANBURY, CONNECTICUT

Contents

Introduction

It's 1269. You are a servant for the Polo family, wealthy merchants in the great Italian trading port of Venice. You've grown up as companion to young master Marco, who's 15 now—just a bit younger than you.

Marco's mother is dead and his father, Niccolò, has not been seen for years. He sailed away on a trading trip with his brother Maffeo. That was about ten years ago. After all this time, most people assume that they're dead. Imagine the thrill, then, when they suddenly reappear—and with an amazing story to tell!

It's the beginning of a great adventure for you and Marco, one that takes you to places you had no idea existed. But if you'd known how dangerous it would be, and that you'd be away for more than 20 years, would you really have wanted to explore with Marco Polo?

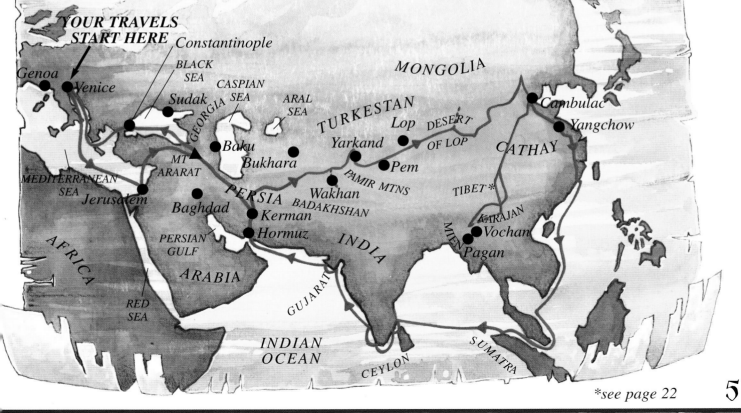

YOUR TRAVELS START HERE

Genoa · Venice · Constantinople · BLACK SEA · Sudak · CASPIAN SEA · GEORGIA · ARAL SEA · MONGOLIA · TURKESTAN · Lop · DESERT OF LOP · Cambulac · Yangchow · Baku · Bukhara · Yarkand · Pem · CATHAY · MT ARARAT · Wakhan · PAMIR MTNS · TIBET * · MEDITERRANEAN SEA · Jerusalem · PERSIA · BADAKHSHAN · KARAJAN · Baghdad · Kerman · Vochan · AFRICA · Hormuz · INDIA · MIEN · Pagan · PERSIAN GULF · ARABIA · GUJARAT · RED SEA · INDIAN OCEAN · CEYLON · SUMATRA

*see page 22

An Unexpected Return

Niccolò

Maffeo

Marco

Over dinner, you hear the brothers' story. First they went to the great trading center of Constantinople,* where Arab dealers bring goods from eastern lands. Then Niccolò and Maffeo decided to try trading in Mongol territory to the northeast, despite knowing next to nothing about these lands. Local wars then forced them to travel into central Asia. From there they went on to Cathay,** a vast land in the distant east. They met its mighty ruler, Kublai Khan, supreme lord of all the Mongols. He has given the Polos a message for their supreme lord, the pope, and sent them home to deliver it.

*present-day Istanbul, in Turkey
**China

The Brothers' Story

FROM CONSTANTINOPLE, the Polos sailed their galley across the Black Sea to the city of Sudak. Here, like other Venetians, they had a trading depot.

THE LANDS BEYOND SUDAK are ruled by the Mongols, a warlike people who control most of Asia. War between rival Mongol rulers blocked the Polos' way home.

The khan gave us this golden passport—it gives us safe passage throughout his empire.

This is you!

Handy Hint

Keep your plans flexible. If you can't travel by one route, try another.

That must be worth a fortune!

I have all the right connections.

THE POLOS had to make a huge detour east. After much hard travel, they reached the city of Bukhara. Here they met an envoy to the court of Kublai Khan, who offered to take them to the khan.

IT TOOK A YEAR, but at last they knelt before the Mongol ruler. He was very curious about the lands they came from and asked many questions about their Christian religion.

SLOWED by blizzards and swollen rivers, the return has taken them three years. Now they learn that the pope has died. They cannot deliver the khan's message until a new pope has been elected.

Setting Off

The khan has asked the pope for holy oil from Jerusalem and a hundred learned men to teach him all about the West. A new pope is chosen in 1271.

Now Niccolò and Maffeo can finally return to Cathay, with papal gifts and greetings. They decide to take Marco with them, and you can't believe your luck when Marco asks you to come along!

After collecting the holy oil from Jerusalem, you head north and east to avoid Egyptian invaders. Then you start the dusty journey southward through Persia.* The route is unsafe. Each village you pass through supplies an escort to the next village—but can you trust the escort?

*now Iran

Chatter!

Quiver!

I just remembered something I have to do at home.

THE POPE has been unable to muster a hundred learned men. He's sent only two friars. They don't get far. The trip has barely started when you learn that invaders from Egypt are ravaging the area just ahead. The cowardly friars flee for home at once.

YOU PASS MOUNT ARARAT in Lesser Armenia.* According to tradition, this is where Noah's ark landed—but you can't find it.

*now part of Turkey

Splash!

Handy Hint

That oil that comes out of the ground is good for treating mange in camels.

It's true! I feel much better now.

AT BAKU near the Georgian border, oil gushes from the ground! You can't use it for cooking, but it burns well in lamps.

20 percent off—that's my last offer.

This way, masters!

AFTER CROSSING miles of desert prickly with thorn bushes, you reach the city of Kerman, famous for the turquoise mined nearby. The Polos do some successful haggling.

9

Bringers of Darkness

You've joined a caravan of merchants, because it's safer to stick with other people. South of Kerman you enter a danger zone where people live at the mercy of bandits called the Karaunas.

Some people believe the Karaunas can use sorcery to create darkness whenever they wish. Sure enough, the sky suddenly grows dark* and the bandits attack you. You, the Polos, and only three other travelers escape. The rest are either killed or sold as slaves.

Fat-tailed sheep

YOU ESCAPE the Karaunas by fleeing to a nearby town.

All the towns and villages of the region have massive walls to keep marauders out. Even so, the local people never feel safe. Once outside the town walls, their animals may be seized, their elders killed, and their children dragged off into slavery.

> I don't think they like the look of us.

> Let us in! Please!

*The darkness may have been caused by "dry fog"—very tiny bits of sand suspended in the air.

10

THE BEASTS people keep here are quite different from those at home. The sheep are as tall as donkeys and store vast amounts of fat in their tails. Beautiful white oxen with humps on their shoulders will kneel down to be loaded.

White ox

Handy Hint

Marco says those fat-tailed sheep are delicious.

Mmmm!

Well, I don't like the look of them!

Shaky Ships

That's better!

You've reached Hormuz, a busy port on the Persian Gulf where all sorts of precious goods from India and Africa arrive. Niccolò and Maffeo Polo plan to board a ship there and travel to Cathay by sea. They think this will be quicker than the land route. As you near the coast, the heat gets worse and worse. By March, every leaf around Hormuz has shriveled.

A SCORCHING WIND from the plains blows over Hormuz in summer. It gets so unbearably hot that people survive by staying neck-deep in water.

Snap!

THEY SAY that an army was caught by this wind and the soldiers shriveled to death. The corpses were so dry that when people tried to move them, the arms snapped off.

MARCO falls ill. You are all worried about him, but Niccolò and Maffeo are also anxious about their goods. The ruler of Hormuz seizes the property of foreigners who die there.

YOU'LL BE GLAD to leave Hormuz. The city is filled with a constant wailing noise. Whenever there is a death, the women of the family mourn loudly every day for four years. The crying never stops.

Waah!

At the docks, the Polos get a shock. To a Venetian, the local ships don't look safe at all. Their planks aren't nailed down; they're stitched together with coconut fiber. And there's no deck—just skins thrown over the cargo. The Polos won't risk crossing the ocean in one of these ships, and that means turning back.

Handy Hint

Avoid the local bread. The brackish water gives it a nasty taste.

The finest ship afloat! I only wish I could go with you...

On the Roof of the World

You have to go back to Kerman to join the land route, which leads you over the barren plains of central Persia and into Turkestan, where chains of mountains stretch in all directions. Marco soon recovers in the fresh mountain air.

In Turkestan you're climbing all the time. You never could have imagined paths so steep. You finally reach a wide, grassy plateau, high in the Pamir Mountains. It must be the top of the world! It will take 12 days to cross, and you'll have to carry everything you need—no merchants live in these heights. It's bitterly cold and there's less oxygen at this height, which is why you can't get the fire to burn well. The flames are so feeble that the stew won't cook. The others are impatient for their meal, but the meat's going to be tough.

MUCH OF THE ROUTE is desert. There's no drinkable water and, worse still, you have to ride a camel. They've got bad tempers and foul breath, and riding one makes you feel seasick.

Where do you think you're going?

IN BADAKHSHAN (a region in Turkestan) rubies are mined, but only for the king. Anyone caught exporting them is executed!

FROM BADAKHSHAN, you follow the Oxus River up through many narrow passes into Wakhan, the gateway to the Pamirs.

DANGEROUS WOLVES lurk in the Pamirs. At night you see their eyes glittering in the light of the campfire.

PAMIR WILD SHEEP* have enormous horns. Their bones are everywhere because the wolves kill them.

*sometimes called Marco Polo sheep

Handy Hint

Your camels may be willing to drink from a brackish water supply if you add flour to it.

I've really worked up an appetite.

I'm doing my best to get the fire going.

PFFFF!!!

15

The Great Desert of Lop

Now you really wish you'd stayed in Venice. In the town of Lop, they warned you about this terrible desert.* They say it's full of evil spirits that fill the air with noises: music, drums, the clash of weapons, and the thunder of galloping horses. Phantom voices call travelers by name, luring them away so they are never seen again.** You're too afraid to look back, but you're sure the demons are right behind you. You can hear them distinctly. You can't imagine how you're going to put up with another month of this—but that's how long it's going to take to cross this desert.

IN THE PROVINCE OF YARKAND, beyond the Pamirs, many people seem to have one foot that's larger than the other. Many also suffer from a goiter (a neck swelling). Marco thinks this is caused by something in the water.***

*now called the Gobi Desert
**The noises are caused by the slipping of sand on the dunes; they can be quite loud and eerie.
***Goiters are often caused by a lack of iodine in the body.

Poor things!

Got one!

IN THE REGION OF PEM you can find lumps of jade in the riverbeds if you search carefully.

Howl!

Handy Hint

Before you go to bed, point a sign in the direction you're traveling— the wind will erase your tracks during the night.

Pull yourself together, man. It's all in your imagination.

Neat!

Ting!

A GUIDE tells you to hang bells on your animals. Otherwise you'll never find them if they stray. Shifting desert sands will hide their tracks.

BEYOND THE DESERT you reach the first Chinese villages. Marco is fascinated by a huge statue of the Buddha.

17

Before the Khan

As soon as he hears that the Polos are in Cathay, Kublai Khan sends escorts to bring your party to him. The khan's presence is awe-inspiring. He sits with a live tiger at his feet. He takes the pope's gifts graciously but is disappointed that there are no learned men traveling with you. He had hoped to learn about the politics, religions, and sciences of other lands. He understands that knowledge is power!

BEFORE they conquered China, the Mongols were herdsmen wandering the Asian steppes. Their portable homes were made of animal skins.

NOW the Mongols live in luxury. The khan has many palaces and even a portable bamboo hunting lodge (above) that looks just like a palace.

At Your Majesty's service!

Handy Hint

Don't tread on the threshold of the khan's Great Hall. It causes bad luck—and you'll get a beating.

THE KHAN loves all kinds of hunting, especially falconry. He rides to the hunt in a pavilion carried by elephants.

IT IS SAID that the khan's magicians can make the weather do whatever he wants, and that they can make his drinking cup float to him through the air.

At least she's quieter than the last one.

IN ADDITION to four official wives, the khan has countless carefully chosen concubines. The ladies of the court check each candidate to ensure that she has sweet breath and does not snore.

19

The Wonderful City

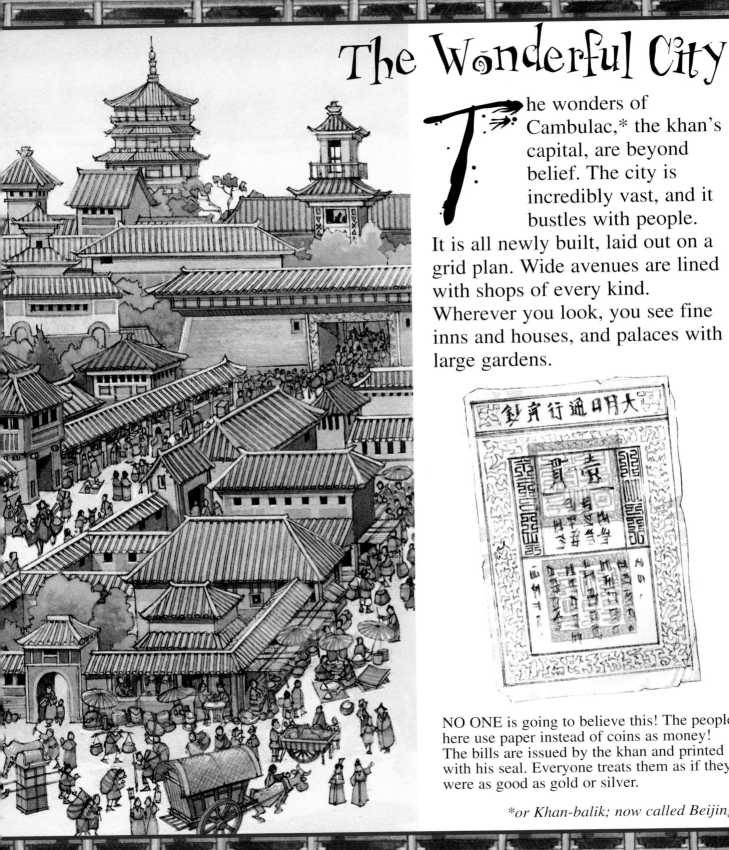

The wonders of Cambulac,* the khan's capital, are beyond belief. The city is incredibly vast, and it bustles with people. It is all newly built, laid out on a grid plan. Wide avenues are lined with shops of every kind. Wherever you look, you see fine inns and houses, and palaces with large gardens.

NO ONE is going to believe this! The people here use paper instead of coins as money! The bills are issued by the khan and printed with his seal. Everyone treats them as if they were as good as gold or silver.

or Khan-balik; now called Beijing

Cambulac makes you feel ashamed of Venice's crooked alleys and smelly canals. And as for wealth—no one at home could imagine the amount of trade that goes on here. Every day 1,000 cartloads of raw silk are brought to the city for weaving, and all the treasures of India and Cathay—precious stones, pearls, the finest cloths—flood into its markets.

Handy Hint

Don't go out at night after the great bell has rung, or you'll be jailed as a suspicious person.

THE KHAN'S VAST PALACE complex contains many buildings, roofed with tiles as bright as crystal. The reception hall is covered with gold and silver and painted dragons. It's so big that 6,000 people can feast inside.

We could use some of this back home.

THE CITY WALLS are 24 miles (39 km) around, with 12 well-guarded gates. Each of the 12 districts inside the walls is bigger than all of Venice.

ANOTHER SURPRISE: black stones that burn like logs and stay lit all night. They are used to heat water in bathhouses. People here take at least three baths a week!

THE POSTAL SERVICE is a wonder. Europe has nothing like it. Riders doing 25-mile (40-km) relays deliver urgent messages. Runners carry ordinary mail.

Marco's Missions

The khan was impressed by the lively way Marco described your journey. Observant people are useful to him. The khan needs to keep firm control of all the lands he's conquered, and for that he needs good information. So he has kept the Polos in his service, and for some years now he has been sending Marco to distant regions to make detailed reports of what he finds. Now Marco and you are on a trip to Tibet, Karajan, and Mien.*

*Tibet is modern Szechwan (Sichuan), Karajan is Yunnan, and Mien is Burma (Myanmar). The country that is now called Tibet is an entirely different place, and Marco didn't go there.

IN TIBET there are forests of giant bamboo canes. You try cutting some for firewood. When lit, the green canes explode with such deafening bangs that your horses bolt! Next time, you tether and blindfold the horses before you light the fire.

IN KARAJAN there are huge serpents* that can eat you in one gulp. The serpents can be killed by sinking blades in the ground, which slit their bellies as they crawl along.

*Today we call them crocodiles!

AT VOCHAN, when a woman has a baby, her husband takes it to bed with him. He stays there for 40 days while his wife waits on him and does all her usual work.

KUIJU PROVINCE* is full of tigers that swim out and snatch fishermen from their boats.
*Historians are not sure where this was.

The gold and silver temples at Pagan, in Mien

Handy Hint

Drinking the bile of those man-eating serpents is said to cure the bite of a mad dog.

And I used to think Venice had all the best buildings!

23

A Voyage to India

As the years go by, you begin to wonder whether Marco ever plans to go home. His career in the khan's service has really taken off. He was made governor of the city of Yangchow for three years, and he's been sent on all sorts of missions. You're with him now on a trip that's brought you to Sumatra and India. Among many other wonders you meet a unicorn*—but it's nothing like the gentle creature that people back home imagine!

Today we know this was really a rhinoceros.

The omens are fine. Can I come down now?

Snort!

YOU'VE COME FROM CATHAY by ship. The crew wouldn't have set off without checking the omens. They tied a man to a kite and launched him from their ship. He didn't crash, so the omens were good.

THERE'S A REALLY YUMMY sweet in Sumatra, made from stuff called sago. It comes from the soft spongy part of a palm tree.

UGH! Creepy crawlies! In India, people hoist their beds to the ceiling with ropes to escape tarantulas.

24

This really isn't how I imagined them at all!

MARCO ADMIRES the Indian yogis (below), who go naked and live on rice. They will not kill any living thing. The Yogis won't even eat leaves unless they are withered, because they say all fresh things have souls.

OYSTERS with magnificent pearls are found in the gulf between India and Ceylon.* Divers hold their breath to the bursting point to bring them up.

now Sri Lanka

Escorting the Princess

After 17 years in the Kublai Khan's service, you are all anxious to get home. But that doesn't suit the khan; he's refusing to let such useful servants go. You're beginning to think you'll be prisoners forever, but then something happens to make him change his mind. The khan of Persia asks for a royal princess to be sent to him as a bride. She must be safely escorted to Persia. Kublai Khan reluctantly decides that the Polos, who are experienced travelers, are needed for the task.

Trust them, my dear.

THE KHAN provides a fleet of 14 ships to carry the princess and her attendants. There are 600 people aboard when you set sail, but only 16 will survive the terrible three-year voyage.

Handy Hint

If you see smoke on the horizon, watch out! It means a pirate ship has spotted you and is signaling others to join the attack.

THE FLEET is marooned for five months in Sumatra, waiting for favorable winds. Some of the islanders are said to be cannibals. You build a stockade on the beach to keep them out, just in case it's true.

DISEASE AND DISASTERS plague the voyage. Crossing the Indian Ocean, you are at the mercy of pirates from the Gujarat Coast, who comb the seas in well-organized fleets.

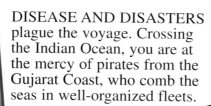

Gulp!

I don't believe it, either.

A NASTY PIRATE TRICK! Merchants who may have swallowed gems to hide them are forced to drink a mixture of tamarind and seawater until they vomit them up.

HERE'S A TALE you find hard to believe, even though sailors swear it's true. On islands off the coast of Africa, there are gigantic birds that prey on elephants. They kill them by dropping them from the sky.

27

Home at Last!

The trip home was not a total disaster. The princess was safely delivered, and after 24 years, you are in back in Venice. People stare at your weather-beaten faces and travel-stained Mongol clothes. When the Polos knock on the door of their house, they are told to go away! It takes time to convince the family that they are the long-lost Niccolò, Maffeo, and Marco, returned as rich men from serving the ruler of half the world. Who's going to believe such stories?

Oh no, you're not!

Oh yes, we are!

Knock knock!

SOME OF MARCO'S SOUVENIRS: silky yak's hair, the dried head and feet of a musk deer, and seeds of Sumatran indigo (Marco planted them but they didn't grow).

Handy Hint

When you've seen wonders that are almost beyond belief, don't get too upset if people won't believe you.

SOME SAY that Marco stunned his doubting family by slitting pouches in his traveling clothes and spilling out cascades of precious stones.

MARCO LATER DICTATED an account of his travels (during his prison stay in Genoa). People say that it's a lot of boasting. Well, some of it may be, but a lot of it is true—you were there!

Right: Chapter 24...

Glossary

Bile A green, bitter liquid produced by a small gland just below the liver.

Brackish Slightly salty and unpleasant to drink.

Buddha The name given to Siddhartha Gautama, the Indian teacher who founded the religion of Buddhism.

Caravan A group of merchants traveling together for safety.

Cathay In Marco Polo's time, a name for what is now northern China.

Concubine A secondary wife, of inferior status to a main wife.

Depot A storehouse for goods.

Envoy A person sent to deliver an official message or to discuss a matter on behalf of the sender.

Falconry Using trained hawks to hunt birds and small mammals.

Galley A long boat with oars, used in ancient times.

Goiter A swelling of the thyroid gland in the neck, often caused by a lack of iodine in the body.

Holy oil Oil blessed by a bishop and used in certain Christian sacraments (rites).

Indigo A plant that produces a highly valued blue dye.

Jade A pale green gemstone.

Khan The title given to the ruler of some Asian countries.

Kublai Khan (1215–1294) Mongol emperor and grandson of Genghis Khan. He extended Mongol rule into southern China and adopted the highly civilized Chinese way of life.

Mange A skin disease of hairy animals, caused by parasitic mites.

Marauders A group of traveling thieves.

Mongols Nomadic herdsmen from central Asia who united in the early 13th century under the conquering warlord Genghis Khan. They created one of the largest empires in history. It stretched from the Pacific Ocean to the Black Sea.

Musk deer A small Asian deer that has no antlers.

Omen An object or event that is supposed to be a sign of future good or evil.

Pamir Mountains A mountain range in Central Asia that includes some of the highest mountains on Earth. After Marco Polo's time, they were not explored by Westerners till 1871.

Pavilion A large, extravagant tent.

Pope The head of the Roman Catholic Church.

Seal A design stamped on documents to prove that they were issued by the seal's owner.

Steppes Vast, treeless plains of northern Asia.

Tamarind Acid-tasting pulp from the pods of the tamarind tree.

Tarantula A name applied to various kinds of large spiders.

Turkestan The historical name of a vast central Asian region that includes modern Turkmenistan, Tajikistan, Uzbekistan, and a part of western China.

Turquoise A blue-green gemstone.

Yak An Asian wild ox with long hair that hangs almost to the ground.

Yogi A person who lives by the principles of Yoga, a branch of the Hindu religion that teaches that inner peace comes from relaxing the body and mind.

Index